'N Sync

Billboard

Created in 1998 by Virgin Books
an imprint of Virgin Publishing Ltd
Thames Wharf Studios
Rainville Road
London
W6 9HT

First published in the United States in 1998 by Billboard Books, an
imprint of BPI Communications Inc., at 1515 Broadway, New York, NY
10036.

Library of Congress Cataloging-in-Publication Data for this title can be
obtained from the Library of Congress.

ISBN 0-8230-8352-7

Printed and bound by Butler & Tanner Ltd, Frome & London

Designed by **nim** Design, London

Colour Reproduction by Colourwise Ltd, Sussex

First printing 1998

'N Sync

ANGIE NICHOLS

Contents

Getting

'N Sync

Every now and again, a city somewhere in the world becomes the birthplace of the latest trend in popular music. Liverpool, England did it back in the 1960s when the Beatles raised the flag of the British pop music invasion of America. A decade later in the 1970s, New York became the gateway for the disco movement. In the 1980s, Seattle, Washington fueled radio airwaves around the world as native bands such as Nirvana and Soundgarden introduced music lovers to the dark angst of grunge. In the late 1990s, the spotlight has turned to Orlando, Florida, and the powerful dance grooves and heavenly harmonies of the male vocal groups 'N Sync and Backstreet Boys.

How did the land of tourist hotels, theme parks and Mickey Mouse do it? Well, like Backstreet Boys before them, the members of 'N Sync were drawn to Orlando for the opportunities it provides for people who love to sing and dance. In the mid 1990s, JC Chasez and Justin Timberlake both found a place to hone their talents on the cable television series *The Mickey Mouse Club*. Across town, Joey Fatone and Chris Kirkpatrick were employed as entertainers at Universal Studios Florida theme park. Chris found his niche as a member of a 1950s-style *a cappella* group, while Joey sang and danced on stage dressed in a monster costume as part of the *Beetlejuice Graveyard Review*. Only the fifth and last member to join the group, Lance Bass, claimed no ties to Orlando prior to joining 'N Sync.

Credit for the creation of 'N Sync belongs to Chris, the group's oldest member, who grew tired of waiting for his lucky break and decided to start his own vocal group. He called up Justin, who was working on *The Mickey Mouse Club* with JC at the time. He also hooked up with Joey, who he knew from their time together at Universal Studios theme park.

When he founded the group in August of 1995, 'N Sync consisted of Justin, Joey, JC, Chris and a fifth friend, who as time went on proved less than committed to long rehearsals and hard work without the guarantee of a recording contract. Needing a replacement, Justin asked the advice of his vocal coach who recommended one of his students, Lance Bass, who fittingly sang in the deep bass voice the group was looking for. Several phone calls and one audition later and 'N Sync had found their final member.

Before the group was signed to a label, the boys rehearsed their harmonizing and dance steps in a large empty warehouse just down the road from the house that JC, Chris, Justin and Justin's mother Lynn shared. It was hard work, with rehearsals sometimes reaching into the late hours of the night. In the first year they were working hard to find management, rehearsing up to four hours a day, while most of the group still held down their day jobs. There's no doubt that the guys knew what they wanted and knew what they had to do to achieve it.

The group performed their first showcase at Walt Disney World's Pleasure Island in October of 1995. That concert, which was filmed for the guys by a friendly former *Mickey Mouse Club* cameraman, became the basis of the promotional video they sent around to record companies and prospective managers.

The guys named their new group 'N Sync at the suggestion of Justin's mother, Lynn, who noted the impressive way the boys were able to sing and dance "in sync." 'N Sync, they later realized, was also an almost perfect acronym using the last letter of each member's first name. N was for Justin; S for Chris; Y as in Joey and C for JC. To make it work out, the boys created a new nickname for Lance. So, N became for Lansten.

'N Sync's promotional video tape attracted the attention of Johnny Wright, the former road manager of the 1980s teen sensation New Kids On The Block and the then manager of Orlando's most famous R&B/pop act, Backstreet Boys. Recognizing 'N Sync's potential, Johnny added the group to the roster of Wright Stuff Management and began shopping his newest discovery around to interested record companies. He never believed there was a conflict of interest working with both Backstreet Boys and 'N Sync. He has said that he was always keen to give fans of vocal groups more variety and more great music.

For their part, 'N Sync felt that the similarities between themselves and Backstreet Boys were mostly superficial, emphasizing the differences between the two bands, their music and particularly their live shows.

Credit for the creation of 'N Sync belongs to Chris, the group's oldest member, who grew tired of waiting for his lucky break and decided to start his own vocal group.

But there is no denying some similarities. Like Backstreet Boys, 'N Sync tapped the talents of several top-name producers such as Full Force and the late Denniz Pop to create their own frothy blend of R&B-charged pop music. The newer group also, like Backstreet Boys, sampled their first taste of true success overseas. In 1997, 'N Sync released their debut CD on BMG Ariola Munich in Germany and Sweden. Both the singles, "Tearin' Up My Heart" and "I Want You Back," became Platinum-selling smashes in each country.

'N Sync began their aural assault on the United States early in 1998 with the release of "I Want You Back." The year turned hectic as the boys toured the country promoting their music at radio stations, county fairs, and malls. Not forgetting their fans in other countries, they also made frequent flights to Europe to help spread their fame to other parts of the continent.

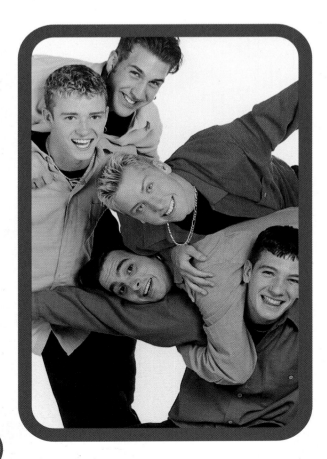

But success didn't really happen in America until 'N Sync received their lucky break from an unexpected source—Backstreet Boys. The elder group had been scheduled that April to film an *In Concert* special for the Disney Channel. When Backstreet Boys cancelled their participation at the last moment, 'N Sync stepped in to take their place. Filmed over the Memorial Day holiday, the show consisted of a live performance by 'N Sync at the Disney-MGM Studios, interviews with the group, and footage of the boys having fun as they rode the attractions at Walt Disney World's Animal Kingdom.

'N Sync's charm and talent proved irresistible. After *'N Sync In Concert* aired for the first time on July 18, 1998, new fans immediately began deluging radio stations, MTV, teen magazines and RCA Records with requests for more information about this suddenly hot new group. Their self-titled CD also began to pick up momentum on Billboard's album charts.

Wisely, 'N Sync continued their promotional efforts as if nothing special was going on around them. They played mini-concerts at Macy's department stores in New York, Boston and Atlanta. When a new Virgin Megastore opened in New York, the group toured the city singing "Tearin' Up My Heart" from the top of a double-decker bus. They sang on talk shows such as *The Tonight Show with Jay Leno* and the morning chat show *The View*. 'N Sync even signed autographs at a promotion for Fetish cosmetics and performed a special concert for winners of a Twix chocolate competition.

And the effort paid off! By September, their self-titled CD had gone double-platinum in the U.S. and Canada. Peaking at number two, it even managed to rise higher than Backstreet Boys' multi-Platinum CD on Billboard's Top 200 album chart.

However successful they'd become, the group barely had time to notice. In October, they performed a month of dates as the opening act for Janet Jackson's *Velvet Rope* tour in select U.S. cities. 'N Sync also rushed back into the studio to record a holiday album. *Home For Christmas*, which was released on November 10, 1998, featured a mix of traditional holiday songs such as "The First Noel" and new romantic Christmas tunes penned specially for the group. In between, they somehow found the time to film three videos: the first to promote their holiday album, another for their third U.S. single "God Must Have Spent A Little More Time On You," and the last, "U Drive Me Crazy," for release in Germany.

Late November found 'N Sync beginning their very first headlining tour of the United States. The boys were also busy filming TV appearances, including *Holiday In Concert* for their friends at Disney Channel. Finally, Thanksgiving morning found the members of 'N Sync braving the chilly weather as they rode a float in Macy's televised parade down New York City's Fifth Avenue.

Whew! Who would have thought that being an overnight sensation was so much work? But what's next for 'N Sync in 1999 and beyond?

One thing's for sure. If they keep making great music and delighting their fans, life will just keep on getting better for these guys.

Did You Know?

The group that most inspires 'N Sync is Boyz II Men ☆ Although 'N Sync are Orlando-based, none of the members are Florida natives ☆ Chris introduced 'N Sync to the golden oldie "The Lion Sleeps Tonight." He used to sing it with his former vocal group, and now 'N Sync frequently perform it in concert ☆ All of the members of 'N Sync bite their fingernails! ☆ These dog-lovers had the bright idea of rescuing a puppy from an animal shelter, taking him on tour and then giving him away to a devoted fan. They hope to put their words into action soon ☆ Three out of the five 'N Sync boys are crazy for basketball. Only Lance and Joey are hopeless at it ☆ If you ask 'N Sync which one of their songs they enjoy singing most, they'll answer "God Must Have Spent A Little More Time On You" ☆ Until 'N Sync's official fan club started, Joey's mother Phyllis stored the band's fan mail in her living room! ☆ None of the 'N Sync guys have steady girlfriends ☆ Before every concert the group members play a game of hackey sack (where they try to keep a little bean bag in the air using only their feet) for good luck ☆

The Boy's Got It!

Justin

With his blue eyes, a head of curly blond hair and a mischievous grin, Justin Randall Timberlake attracts the most frenzied attention from females. It's no wonder: this cute teenager can really turn on the charm. He's funny, smart, talented—and extremely energetic, too!

The baby of the 'N Sync boys was born on January 31, 1981 in Memphis, Tennessee to Lynn and Randy Timberlake. Since his parents split-up and eventually remarried, Justin now regards his step-parents as essential parts of his family. He's also utterly devoted to his two younger half-brothers, Jonathan, who's five, and baby Steven Robert, who was born on August 28, 1998.

Justin discovered his love of singing in church and began taking vocal lessons at the age of eight. His participation in a school play further cemented his love of being on stage. His earliest hopes were to either become a professional singer or a basketball star. Although he's finally given up on the latter, he still plays basketball as much as possible. In fact, the celebrity he'd most like to meet is superstar player Michael Jordan.

MMC Members Only
In 1993, when he was 12, Justin joined the cast of the TV series *The Mickey Mouse Club*. Although the job entailed a move to Orlando, he describes it as one of the smartest choices he's ever made in his life. As one of the gang of young, talented kids on the show, Justin sang, danced and performed comedy skits each episode. Justin has said that this was one of the best things he has ever done,

trying out singing, comedy, and acting without being restricted to one thing. His participation in *MMC* (as it was known to its dedicated fans) even gave Justin a chance to perform before a live audience on the TV special *MMC the Concert*.

This cute teenager can really turn on the charm. He's funny, smart, talented—and extremely energetic, too!

Despite the almost five-year difference in their ages, Justin became very close pals with fellow *MMC* member JC Chasez. The boys were often teamed up for comedy sketches and musical numbers. Even after *MMC* was cancelled in October of 1994, the pair kept in touch. For a time, they were both living in Memphis, Tennessee working with the same vocal coach and writers on separate solo projects. Not long after, Justin moved back to Orlando where he received the invitation from Chris to become a participant in a new vocal group. It was only natural that he should think to include his friend JC too.

Baby Blue

The key to really getting to know Justin is keeping in mind his three passions: 'N Sync, sports and shopping!

For this blond-haired teenager, nothing beats the thrill of performing with 'N Sync, particularly when they're singing with a live band. He's said that one of the best things about playing with real musicians rather than a backing tape is the way the band can change the tempo a little to make every performance different.

Justin finds the unpredictable nature of a live performance very exciting. In the best sense, it lends an electric anticipation in the moments before a show. That burst of adrenaline when 'N Sync hit the stage is the feeling that Justin lives for. As the show wears on and the crowds' love pours back in waves of cheering and applause, all the hard work and sacrifice is forgotten. He has said that he sees a 'N Sync gig as like a big party with a lot of friends. No 'N Sync fan would ever disagree!

That burst of adrenaline when 'N Sync hit the stage is the feeling that Justin lives for.

Unfortunately, the not-so-good thing about the unpredictability of a live performance is that things can go terribly wrong. Although everyone in the group has confessed to moments when he's forgotten a dance step or missed his cue in a song, sometimes it can get downright dangerous on stage. Justin learned this lesson first hand in 1997 when he broke his thumb during a performance.

"Somebody put some water on the stage. We were doing an outside show and they were hosing down the audience," he remembered during a live Internet chat. "We do this dance move where we slide across the stage and my hand buckled. And I still finished the song!" Despite having to wear a plaster cast on his thumb, Justin was able to continue 'N Sync's European tour. What a trooper! It would take more than a broken bone to keep this energetic teenager down.

Naturally athletic Justin is an avid basketball player. Although JC and Chris also share his devotion to the sport, they all admit that Justin has the best slam dunk among them. Just about all of his free time away from 'N Sync is spent shooting hoops or watching a game on television. When they're at home in Orlando, JC, Chris and Justin play almost every day in their backyard, where they have a real basketball court. Although his height is impressive—he's actually the tallest member of 'N Sync at 6ft—Justin mourns the fact that he's not big enough to play professional sports.

Like most guys his age, Justin's also an avid video game player. He and the group have carried a Sony PlayStation with them all around the world. What is his number one game? Video basketball, of course!

The 'Sporty Spice' of the group is pretty choosy about the food he eats. Justin doesn't like to pig out on junk food like McDonalds, chips and sweets; he's much more likely to choose a healthy snack like fruit and a glass of milk. He also loves starchy things like pasta for dinner and cereal for breakfast. Give him a whole box of Apple Jacks cereal and he's in heaven!

Though he's the youngest member of 'N Sync, Justin has an advanced sense of style. He really enjoys dressing up in snazzy suits or teaming trousers with a really great-fitting jacket. He's got the best fashion sense of all the 'N Sync guys. On the casual side, Justin's partial to sports jerseys (particularly North Carolina's baby blue basketball jersey) and designer footwear. He has more than 20 pairs!

When it comes to more intimate wear, Justin has revealed in interviews that he goes for long boxer briefs by Calvin Klein. An admitted shopaholic, Justin has enjoyed visiting clothing shops around the world. Sometimes he's had so much fun that it was difficult for him to fit all his new purchases into his luggage!

"We do this dance move where we slide across the stage and my hand buckled. And I still finished the song!"

Girls, Girls, Girls

The most frequent question that Justin is asked is whether he has a girlfriend. Well, he doesn't—none of the 'N Sync guys do. He also admits that he's never been in love, but he hasn't given up on Cupid's arrow hitting his heart someday.

Justin received his first kiss in grade school from a girl who lived across the street from his best friend. The smooch happened one night while he was over at the girl's house watching television. Justin tells of how she suddenly turned the TV and the lights off, and how the two of them were lost for words, sitting there in the dark. He recalls how he thought he might as well go for it, and found to his delight that it was a great experience!

Though it's hard to believe, Justin's also had his heart broken too. Her name was Danielle and he met her at a *MMC* party in 1995. The two of them immediately felt a connection and dated for nine months. Justin ended the relationship when he found out she was secretly seeing someone else behind his back. He admits the revelation crushed him at the time.

Justin admits that he's never been in love, but he hasn't given up on Cupid's arrow hitting his heart some day.

So what does Justin look for in a girl? Honesty, obviously! Justin also admires girls with a healthy dose of self-confidence, and who can make him laugh. It also helps if a prospective date enjoys the TV series *South Park*, as Justin likes to do frequent imitations of its cartoon characters. He professes not to be overly impressed by a pretty face but is more attracted to someone who's fun to be with, sensitive, and not stuck-up.

He has said that he really hates fake people, and girls who act superior. But if a girl is honest and confident, and he really likes her, he'll go out of his way to sweep her off her feet.

It's no wonder the other members of 'N Sync have nicknamed Justin 'Mr. Smooth'!

If a girl is honest and confident, and he really likes her, he'll go out of his way to sweep her off her feet.

21

Justin
The Secret File

As a member of *The Mickey Mouse Club*, Justin had the chance to visit Walt Disney World often. His number one ride is Space Mountain ☆ Girls love it, but Justin professes to hate his curly hair ☆ Justin thinks it would be fun to perform a duet with teenage country music singer LeAnn Rimes ☆ At home, Justin's room is filled with 1970s artifacts like incense burners and funky candles ☆ He's terrified of snakes! ☆ His other nicknames include Baby, Curly, Shot and Bounce ☆ The singer Justin admires most is Stevie Wonder ☆ Justin drives a ruby-red Mercedes Benz M-class with lots of chrome extras! ☆ Hip-hop and R&B artists like Take 6, Dru Hill, Boyz II Men and Brian McKnight come top of Justin's hit list ☆ Justin's grouchy in the morning until after he eats his breakfast ☆ When he's in the U.S., Justin tries to catch the repeats of *Seinfeld*—he reckons it's the best thing on TV ☆ The Beach Boys were the headliners at the first concert that Justin ever attended ☆

Joey

Life In The Spotlight

Though he left the Brooklyn area he once called home as a teenager, Joseph Anthony Fatone Jr.'s personality still retains that legendary New York charm. Confident, talkative, flirtatious, good-natured and a little bit of a wise guy—it's no wonder that so many 'N Sync fans around the world have taken Joey to their hearts.

It's no wonder that so many 'N Sync fans around the world have taken Joey to their hearts.

Born on January 28, 1977, Joey grew up in a home where music played a large role. His father, Joseph Fatone Sr., used to sing professionally with a group called the Orions. The group put out some records but never achieved worldwide fame; however, they inspired Joey and his siblings to pursue the creative arts.

Joey remembers that every time they played, he and his sister would sing and dance backstage, imitating his dad's dance routines.

And while Joey remains the most famous member of his family today, he's not the only one making a living as a performer. His older sister Janine, who's 26, is also a singer, while his brother Steven, 24, dances with a group called Solid Harmonie.

Super Joey

Tired of New York's long cold winters and troubled by the changes they saw in their native Brooklyn, Joseph and Phyllis Fatone moved their family to sunny Orlando, Florida when their youngest son was 13 years old. Cute Joey, who loved commanding the spotlight from the time he first learned to talk, attended Dr. Phillips High School in Orlando, a performing arts school. It was there that he first got involved in dancing, trying out jazz, ballet and even tap.

Joey also started making the rounds of auditions. His persistence was rewarded when he won small roles in the feature films *Once Upon A Time In America* and *Matinee*. Joey even guest-starred on an episode of the science fiction television series *seaQuest DSV*.

After earning his high school diploma, Joey found a steady job at Universal Studios Florida theme park. As a member of the *Beetlejuice Graveyard Review*, Joey sang rock music dressed up as famous movie monsters. Depending on his schedule, he appeared as the Wolfman, Dracula or the Phantom of the Opera. While the *Beetlejuice Graveyard Review* was a long way from Broadway, Joey really enjoyed the interaction with the audience, the lights and special effects and the chance to dazzle everyone with his singing and fancy dance steps. Although no one could tell who he was under his monster costume,

No matter how tired this brown-eyed performer is, he's perpetually cheerful, armed with a ready smile and an easy laugh.

it definitely beat waiting tables as he looked for his big break in showbiz.

Of course, it was at Universal Studios that Joey met Chris, who was singing doo-wop-style 1950s songs with a group called the Hollywood Hightones. The pair shared a similar outlook on life, a love of vocal groups and a passion for Orlando's vibrant club scene. They became such good friends that when Chris decided to start a group of his own, he invited Joey to join the fold.

Ladies' Man
Aside from the vocal and dance talents he brings to 'N Sync, Joey has a much-appreciated gift for cheering up the other members of the group. No matter how tired this brown-eyed performer is, he's perpetually cheerful, armed with a ready smile and an easy laugh.

Although no one could tell who he was under his monster costume, it definitely beat waiting tables as he looked for his big break in showbiz.

Joey's knack for easy conversation and good-natured jokes has not gone unnoticed by the female population of the world. He's the group's biggest flirt who claims he's rarely troubled by shy moments, and has been nicknamed 'chick magnet' by Chris.

The boy simply can't help it! Whether he's chatting with a timid pre-teen 'N Sync fan or the 80-year-old grandmother of a friend, there's a grin on his face and a twinkle in his eyes.

Born with a natural gift for gab, Joey could probably coax a mountain lion to roll over and purr!

He loves women of every age, shape and size. And no, Joey doesn't have a girlfriend either.

"We're single and ready to mingle," he announced on behalf of the entire group during an appearance on MTV.

But however much he flirts, it's a rare occasion when Joey actually gets the girl! 'N Sync's busy schedule is certainly part of the reason, but he also speculates that because he flirts with everyone, few girls take his interest seriously. Poor Joey!

He's especially attracted to girls who are friendly and face the world with a confident smile. A girl who displays a bit of rhythm on the dancefloor will definitely catch his eye too because Joey loves to go out clubbing! Like Justin, Joey has a problem with people who pretend to be someone they're not. Phonies and pretentious divas need not apply. Most of all, Joey's attracted to a girl who can just be herself and have fun!

Joey experienced his first kiss from a girl who lived nearby named Lisa. She wasn't a girlfriend but merely a pal when a bunch of their friends locked the two of them in a dark closet together. While it's likely that neither Joey nor Lisa remembers the moment as the most romantic kiss of their lives, it was all in good fun. In fact, when Joey goes and visits his friends and relatives who still live in his home town, he often runs into Lisa, who remains a friend.

Aside from women and 'N Sync, the other passion in Joey's life is the comic-book Man of Steel, Superman. He collects absolutely everything related to the character and has even been known to wear a contact lens emblazoned with the famous Superman logo! From T-shirts and books to toys and rings, Joey's built up quite a collection. Since becoming famous, Joey has seen his Superman collection grow even larger. His home now boasts a whole new bookcase to house the Superman gifts he's received from fans.

Club Style

When it comes to style, Joey often marches to the beat of his own drummer, which is not necessarily easy to do when your group's image is clean-cut and wholesome. In the early years of 'N Sync, Joey argued with the group's management to let him keep his goatee beard and pierced eyebrow. He lost the piercing and even shaved his beard for a while, but he's finally been able to grow it back.

Joey essentially sports a club look, but some of the more peculiar items in his wardrobe have become the butt of the other guys' jokes. They always comment on his clothes when they're on tour, and reckon Joey's hairy coat and matching boots make him look like Chewbacca. From enormous red suits to trousers that light up, Joey's closet is filled with lots of surprises. Chris has said that Joey does have a sense of style, but one that's crazy and off-the-wall.

Like his fashion sense, Joey's interests are very diverse. He's equally at home sitting in front of the TV laughing over the mischief of the cartoon *South Park* as he is spending some quiet time rereading William Shakespeare's *Macbeth*. He'll dance all night but he doesn't really enjoy any sport but in-line skating.

If a girl really wants to impress Joey, the way to his heart is through his taste buds. But beware, there's quite a culinary standard to live up to! Joey's mother is a fabulous cook and he

misses her home-cooked meals tremendously when he's on the road. With a nod to his Italian heritage, he loves to eat lasagna, pasta and almost anything in a tomato sauce.

For the future, Joey plans to make the most of his time with 'N Sync. He loves travel, performing on stage and learning new dance routines. He especially enjoys meeting fans and making new friends of the other musicians he meets on the road. Some of his closest new pals in the industry are Lene Grawford Nystrom of Aqua, former Spice Girl Geri Halliwell and the four members of up-and-coming group 98°. Like most of the guys in 'N Sync, Joey's also extremely excited about

becoming more involved in the writing, choreography and studio production duties for their group.

On the personal front, Joey definitely plans to settle down with a wife and kids of his own some day. He's an extremely family-oriented person who dreams of a time when he can fill an Orlando home of his own with lots of love and good music.

Joey does have a sense of style, but it's crazy and off-the-wall.

Joey
The Secret File

If he could sit down for a chat with simply anyone from any time, he'd pick the Bard himself, William Shakespeare ☆ Joey says his biggest fault is that he can be a little lazy ☆ Joey's loves anything purple ☆ This family-oriented guy has often invited his older siblings and his parents to join 'N Sync during their travels around the world ☆ Though he loves all sorts of music, Joey has a special affection for the romantic harmonies of Boyz II Men and the 1950s group Frankie Lymon and the Teenagers ☆ *Willie Wonka and the Chocolate Factory* is his number one movie of all time ☆ Joey wishes his feet were smaller! ☆ Joey loves visiting London, because it has so much history as well as a vibrant music scene ☆ Joey doesn't think he's ever been in love for real, but he did have strong feelings for a girl named Dinay who he dated for four months during high school ☆ Joey's nicknames are Party Animal, Superman and Phat-one ☆ His most embarrassing moment was when he appeared on stage without realizing his pants were unzipped ☆ Joey has had a crush on actress Demi Moore forever! ☆

A Bright Spark

Whether he's dancing, singing, or just having a conversation, Joshua Scott Chasez has a certain charisma that sets him apart from the crowd. He possesses an indefinable quality that's more than the sum of his handsome features. Perhaps it's due to his obvious enjoyment of his work with 'N Sync, the thrill that he feels on stage and the zeal for perfection that he puts into every thought and movement. Of all the members of the group, JC is the most ambitious.

What's surprising is that JC discovered his singing talent relatively late in life. Born on August 8, 1976 in Bowie, Maryland (a suburb of Washington, D.C.) to Roy and Karen Chasez, JC loved to dance and play sports. He excelled at football, basketball and gymnastics—the latter a talent he brings to 'N Sync's stage show through his awe-inspiring somersaults and handstands. But up until his audition for *The Mickey Mouse Club* at age 13, JC had only sung along with the radio while taking a shower.

Up until his audition for The Mickey Mouse Club at age 13, JC had only sung along with the radio while taking a shower.

In The Mouse House Too!

JC's life changed overnight in 1991 when he became a member of the TV variety series *The Mickey Mouse Club*. Over his four seasons on the show, JC performed comedy skits, sang, danced and even got a chance to meet some of his musical idols who guest-starred on episodes, such as Boyz II Men. JC quickly became a hit with the show's fans, too. One of the most popular characters he played was Clarence 'Wipeout' Adams, a funny surfer dude who popped up frequently in sketches.

Most significantly, *The Mickey Mouse Club* afforded JC the opportunity to hone his singing, dancing and stage presence. In 1993, the show's producers released an album of music performed by the cast, aptly titled *MMC*. JC's vocal talents are utilized all over the CD, but he especially shined performing the lead vocals on two songs, "Let's Get Together" and "I Saw Her First." That same year, JC joined the other members of the cast in a mini-concert tour of America. That's where JC discovered the thrill of performing before an audience and decided the course of his future.

After *The Mickey Mouse Club* was cancelled at the end of 1994, JC began making plans for a solo singing career. He worked with a vocal coach and songwriters in Memphis, Tennessee for a while—coincidentally the same people who were working with Justin on his own solo album. However, before either guy landed a record deal of his own, 'N Sync came calling.

For his part, JC has no regrets. Being a member of 'N Sync has made him a bigger star than he ever was on *MMC* and it's given him many opportunities to learn more about the music industry. Often considered the most serious member of the group, JC doesn't fool around in the recording studio or before a show. He's much too busy soaking up every bit of information he can learn from the producers, engineers, and lighting people. Every aspect of the industry fascinates him.

JC loves to have fun, but he's the 'N Sync member most likely to leave a party early to go back to work. He constantly writes songs and hopes to see 'N Sync pen all of their own music someday soon. Since buying a set of keyboards light enough to carry with him on tour, not a day goes by without JC spending at least a few minutes playing. You can bet JC will always be involved in music, either working in the studio or rehearsing for shows—it's just another form of relaxation for him.

Music will always be JC's number one priority, no matter how famous 'N Sync become.

Sleepyhead

JC has often joked that his number one hobby is sleeping. That's because he's the sort of person whose body requires a full eight hours of shut-eye to operate at peak performance. That's unfortunate, because since joining 'N Sync, a full night's sleep is a luxury that's hard to come by!

Fans who come to an 'N Sync show should know that JC has one odd little bedtime habit. After a concert, he'll usually pick one of the stuffed animals that he's been given by his fans to sleep with him. Perhaps they help remind him of his cat Grendal at home?

When JC's not working or sleeping, he likes to spend his time watching movies. Alone in his hotel room, he'll watch as many as three features in a night. He's partial to science fiction and action films such as the *Star Wars* and *Indiana Jones* movies (Harrison Ford is the actor that JC most admires). Other movies he particularly enjoyed recently include *The Fifth Element* and *Blade*.

Because of his appreciation of choreography and fine music, JC takes up every chance he gets to catch shows. Dinner, followed by a musical, followed by a quiet romantic table for

two and a decadent dessert is JC's first choice when it comes to spending time with someone he really likes.

And what kind of girl catches JC's eye? Someone who is confident and unafraid to voice her opinions really rates with him. He also likes girls who can look on the lighter side of life, have an easy-going nature and a ready laugh. Despite the many opportunities he has to meet models, actresses and gorgeous singers, JC's not extremely impressed with physical beauty, and has said that he doesn't like judging people by appearances—inner values are more important. However, only patient girls need apply to JC as date-mates. His schedule with 'N Sync is so busy that sadly, most of JC's recent relationships with girls have been friendships conducted over long-distance phone lines.

He likes girls who can look on the lighter side of life, have an easy-going nature and a ready laugh.

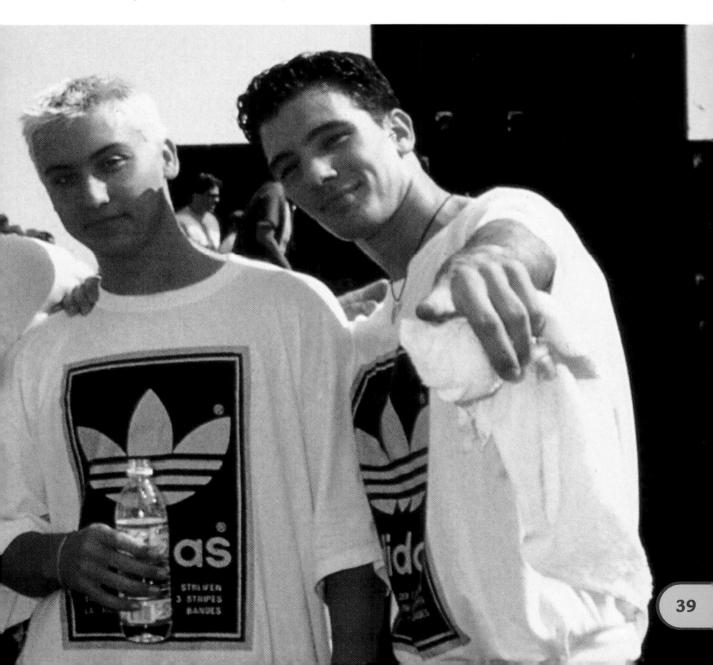

In Private

In terms of style, JC prefers to go casual whenever possible. He's not a great fan of getting dressed up! On a perfect day, he'd wear a comfy pair of jeans, sneakers and an old sweater over a T-shirt. But despite his preferred lived-in look, the other guys in 'N Sync agree that he's the most style-conscious of the bunch. He's not trendy, but rather classic in his taste in clothes.

JC's so finicky about the clothing he wears that his hotel room is often a complete mess! Sometimes he'll try on just about everything in his suitcase-and leave the discards on the floor-before he finds what he wants. For these reasons he's often the last one down to the tour bus in the morning. He admits that his bedroom at home has the same "lived in" look!

At home in Orlando, JC has a vast collection of menus from Hard Rock Cafes all over the world. He's almost managed to paper the walls of his room with them. Oddly, the burgers and fries they serve at the world's Hard Rocks aren't his first choice of a bite to eat. JC's biggest weakness is for Chinese food. When he's out on the road with 'N Sync he'll have it for dinner at least once a week.

What are JC's other passions? The cartoon *South Park*, the Washington Redskins American football team, lying on the beach, and driving his black Jeep Cherokee top his list. JC also has two younger siblings, Heather, who's 20, and his baby brother Tyler, who's not such a baby at age 16. Whenever JC goes home, he loves to spend time with them, making the most of every second of free time.

JC's future is completely wrapped up in succeeding in the music business. Songwriting, producing, choreographing, maybe even managing a new group—he wants to do it all. But right now his ultimate goal is to help make 'N Sync the best-known R&B/pop vocal group in the world. And then? Well, JC still wouldn't mind a solo career some day, but that's a long way off. Though singing remains his first love, he also wouldn't hesitate to give acting another try. He always found that bringing across the emotions of the characters he played was a fascinating process. He'd love to do it again.

For JC, as well as his friends in 'N Sync, the possibilities of the future are limitless.

JC
The
Secret File

Before he moved to Orlando, JC attended a very strict Catholic school in Maryland ☆ His last name is pronounced Shaz-ay ☆ Some of the actresses JC would love to meet are Meg Ryan, Julia Roberts and Halle Berry ☆ Criticism can made JC feel insecure. He tries to deal with it by ignoring unkind comments ☆ An early bloomer, JC had his first girlfriend in the first grade! ☆ Like Joey, JC attended Dr. Phillips High School ☆ Eeek! JC hates going to the doctor because he's scared of needles ☆ Two of JC's most admired musicians are Sting and Seal because of their songwriting brilliance ☆ If he had the chance, JC would wear black all the time ☆ JC still sings in the shower all the time ☆ When he's thirsty, JC reaches for a bottle of iced tea ☆ He says that the best book he has ever read is *The Hobbit* by J.R.R. Tolkien ☆

Lance

Show Stopper

The biggest misconception about 'N Sync's bass singer Lance Bass is that he's extremely shy. It's true, compared to the other motormouths in the group—notably Chris and Joey—Lance is a lot quieter, but he's not exactly bashful. This crooner from Clinton, Mississippi just has a tendency to think carefully before he speaks. And when it comes to the female population, Lance is really not shy at all!

When it comes to the female population, Lance is really not shy at all!

James Lance Bass was born in Laurel, Mississippi on May 4, 1979 to Jim and Diane Bass. He has one older married sister named Stacy, who's not involved in the entertainment industry.

It's actually something of a surprise that Lance became a singer. The importance of a good education was always stressed in his family and Lance was always a good student. Until he joined 'N Sync in his final year of high school, he assumed he'd be headed for a four-year college. In fact, he was thinking about a career in space administration, working for NASA, after he earned his degree. But fate had a different plan for Lance.

Picking up his life and moving to Orlando wasn't easy for Lance at first, but luckily he enjoys a good adventure.

Lucky Break

Like so many other talented kids, Lance first began singing in church, and in his school's chorus. In seventh grade he auditioned and won a part in a state-wide touring group called the Mississippi ShowStoppers. It was a great experience for Lance because he got to travel, meet new people and feel the rush of performing on stage. He loved every moment of it.

In high school, Lance continued to sing and take voice lessons but he never thought he would actually be able to make a living as a performer. He's a very practical person who understood how high the odds were against him. Fortunately, his vocal coach thought otherwise. When another of his teacher's students, 'N Sync's Justin Timberlake, called to ask for a recommendation, he gave him Lance's phone number.

Picking up his life and moving to Orlando wasn't easy for Lance at first, but luckily he enjoys a good adventure. The first year was extremely hectic as he was busy finishing his high school degree through a correspondence course as well as working with the group. He also felt guilty that his parents had uprooted their life in Mississippi to come to Florida with him. He's the first to admit that he would never have come so far without their generous love and support. They'd do anything for their son! So when 'N Sync flew to Europe for several weeks of promotional touring, Lance's mother Diane came along to be his guardian. He was really happy that he could pay her back for all her sacrifices by giving her a chance to see a little of the world.

Eventually, Lance's life settled into a pleasant routine. When he turned 18, his parents moved back home and he found an apartment of his own in Orlando. Oddly, once he was done with his high school courses, Lance found that he missed studying. He's currently taking a college correspondence class in business administration through the University of Nebraska.

Sir Lance

In every successful group, each member plays a defined role. Within 'N Sync, Lance is the organized one who always knows the day's schedule. Nicknamed 'Scoop' by the other boys, Lance is the one everyone turns to when they have a question about the itinerary.

Lance's other defining quality is his laid-back attitude. He rarely gets upset or worried about anything! This green-eyed guy gets dressed in no time every morning. Fussing over clothes just doesn't appeal to him because he just can't be bothered worrying about how he looks. His everyday uniform is jeans or chinos, a T-shirt and sneakers. That's it! Lance also prefers to keep his hair quite short, because it's very thick and hard to style. He likes to do nothing more than wash it and throw a comb through it. Now that's a laid-back guy!

Of course, Lance does care about what he looks like on a date. He really enjoys meeting new people and treating a special girl to a great time. When it comes to meeting girls, Lance tends to watch someone he's interested in and bide his time for the perfect moment to make his move. The other guys in 'N Sync have nicknamed him 'Stealth' because of this tendency to quietly and swiftly sweep a young lady off her feet.

The typical date of dinner and a movie is far too tame for Lance. He much prefers taking a female friend along on an outdoor adventure!

Like the other 'N Sync guys, Lance is pretty athletic. He's not as excited about team sports though—he'd rather go horseback riding, jet-skiing, rock climbing, parasailing or skydiving. A gal needs to be pretty fearless to keep up with Lance! However, when all the day's extreme sports are done, Lance enjoys kicking back on a secluded stretch of beach to share a picnic lunch with someone special. Lance loves the beach!

Aside from a girl with a lust for adventure, Lance looks for women who are smart, somewhat innocent, and down-to-earth. He thinks that Jennifer Aniston, one of the stars of Friends, is gorgeous because of her pretty hair and sweet grin.

In a magazine interview, he admitted that he definitely notices a girl's eyes and smile first. But the things that keeps him interested in a relationship are honesty and trust.

Like the rest of the guys in 'N Sync, Lance is very single these days, but he'd really love to have a girlfriend! It's just that with his crazy schedule, he doesn't think it would be fair to the other person who would be left home alone a lot.

To further prove that Lance is not as shy as he seems, it's important to note that he had his very first girlfriend when he was just a five-year-old at kindergarten! Her name was Bethany Dukes and the first time Lance kissed her was before the whole school at the South Jones High School homecoming dance. On that night, Lance and Bethany were chosen to crown the king and the queen of the dance (it was a tradition to have two of the youngest students from the grammar school present the prize). During the ceremony, right in front of everyone,

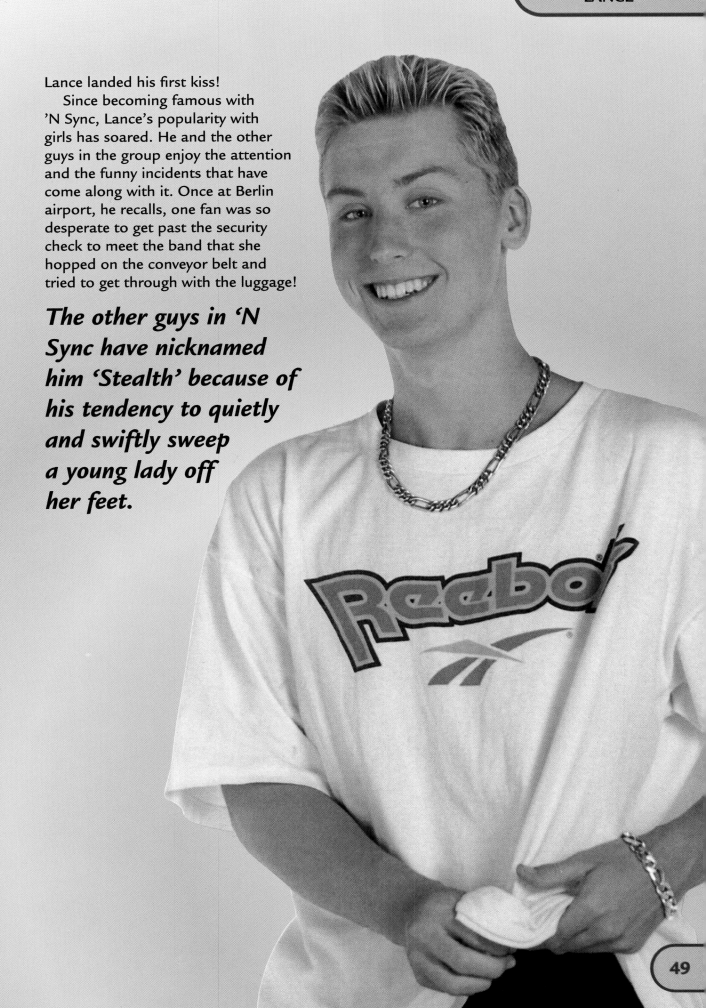

Lance landed his first kiss!

Since becoming famous with 'N Sync, Lance's popularity with girls has soared. He and the other guys in the group enjoy the attention and the funny incidents that have come along with it. Once at Berlin airport, he recalls, one fan was so desperate to get past the security check to meet the band that she hopped on the conveyor belt and tried to get through with the luggage!

The other guys in 'N Sync have nicknamed him 'Stealth' because of his tendency to quietly and swiftly sweep a young lady off her feet.

49

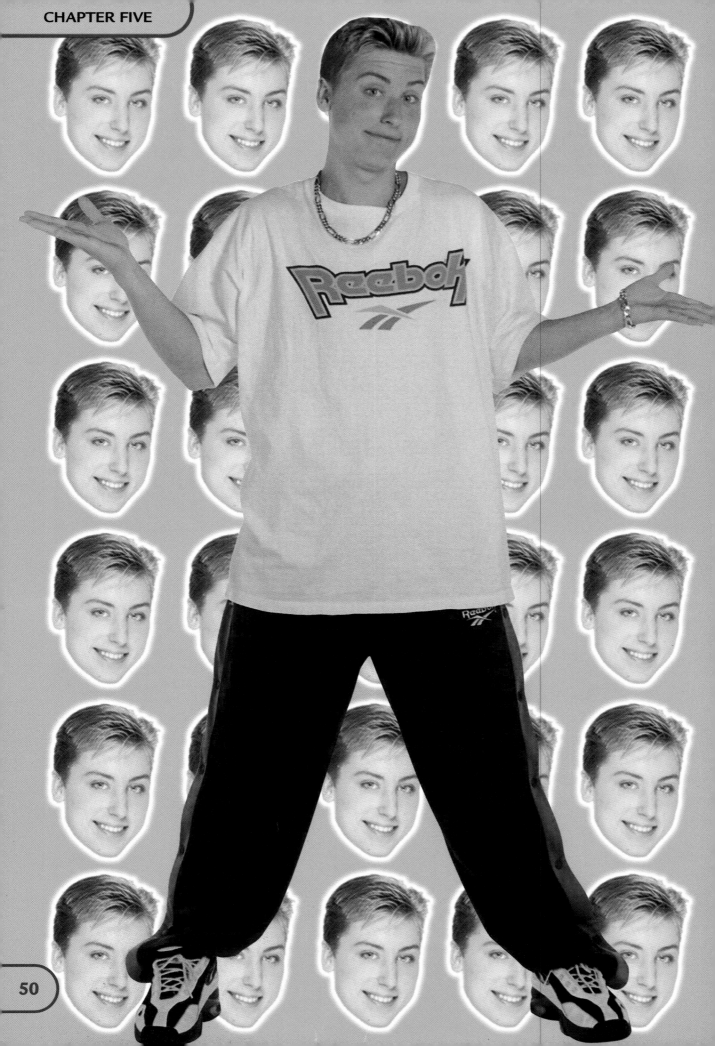

A Bit of Fun

When it comes to music, Lance has some of the most varied taste in 'N Sync. He loves R&B groups like Take 6 and Boyz II Men, but he can also appreciate the hard rock of Offspring and the classic harmony-laden tunes of the Bee Gees. This fan of country crooner Garth Brooks would love to convince 'N Sync to record a new version of his song, "The Dance." Lance also loves music by Matchbox 20, Celine Dion and Aerosmith. Now that's variety!

Lance's top cartoon character is Taz, the Tasmanian Devil from Warner Brothers' cartoons. He collects simply everything with his image on it, from watches to stuffed toys to T-shirts—if it has Taz on it, Lance owns it. He also collects coins, stamps and antiques guns and knives.

Like the other guys in the group, Lance has a talent to entertain. Joey claims that his impression of a squirrel eating a nut is one of the funniest things he's ever seen! During photo shoots, Lance is one of the liveliest members of the group. He's been known to grab odd props like a toy ray gun to point at the photographer or even to chase the other 'N Sync guys around with a dustpan and brush, in a bit of good-natured mischief.

In the future, Lance plans to put his classes in business administration to good use. While JC is excited about learning all of the technical aspects of making music, Lance is much more interested in the financial side. The other members have often commented on his sharp business brain, always coming up with new ideas for merchandise or spin-off projects.

Lance is wary of taking too much credit for the success of 'N Sync, however. He believes that the wonderful things that have happened to the group are a combination of hard work, good luck and the support of an excellent management team. One day, Lance would like to share some of his good fortune and knowledge by helping to manage a group of his own.

On a personal level, Lance plans to buy a ranch with a few horses someday (he loves animals) and to definitely find someone special to gallop with him off into the sunset. Knowing his love for extreme sports, we just hope she's not afraid of heights!

Lance
The Secret File

Lance drives a black Toyota 4-runner ☆ 'N Sync's hectic schedule made Lance decide to find a new home for his puppy ☆ He couldn't care for it, so he gave it to one of his teacher mom's students ☆ For a breakfast treat, Lance prefers French toast over anything ☆ Like the rest of the world, Lance got pretty misty-eyed while watching *Titanic*, and he's not afraid to admit it ☆ When Lance is thirsty he reaches for a Dr. Pepper ☆ Lance wears a horseshoe ring and two WWJD (What Would Jesus Do) bracelets given to him by fans ☆ Lance dislikes mushrooms, rap music and people who prejudge others ☆ Repeats of *I Love Lucy* and the current TV series *Third Rock from the Sun* make Lance laugh ☆ The only team sport that Lance really enjoys is volleyball. Especially when it's played on the beach ☆ Mmmm... Lance's hot drink of choice is an almond cappuccino ☆ Mexican cuisine makes Lance happy ☆

Chris

Dance Dynamo

Life with Chris Kirkpatrick, the oldest member of 'N Sync, is never, ever boring! Born in Clarion, Pennsylvania on October 17, 1971, and raised in Dalton, Ohio, this oldest of five children is never at a loss for words. From earliest childhood he enjoyed attention and spent a lot of time teasing his younger half-sisters Molly, Kate, Emily and Taylor. Raised in a single-parent household by his mother Beverly, Chris recalls that he was always singing and cracking jokes around the house.

Music played a large part in Chris's early years. When other kids turned to CDs, he loyally held on to his records (he still owns a huge collection) and enjoyed DJing at parties. Michael Jackson was a huge early influence and *Thriller* was the very first record he ever bought. Chris loved to imitate Michael's innovative dance moves, too. These days, Chris is the member of 'N Sync who's most in tune with the urban sounds of hip-hop, R&B and rap music. Some current artists on his Walkman include Busta Rhymes, Dru Hill, Boyz II Men and soulful crooner Brian McKnight.

Chris is the member of 'N Sync who's most in tune with the urban sounds of hip-hop, R&B and rap music.

Doo-wop Date

Chris's earliest career goal was to become an actor. After graduating from high school he enrolled in Orlando's Velencia College where he earned an Associate of Arts degree. He later transferred to Rollins College, also in the Orlando area, where he became a part of the school's chamber choir. Performing with the choir, Chris discovered his talent for singing in the high falsetto that's one of the signature sounds of 'N Sync.

To help support him through school, Chris joined the Hollywood Hightones, a group that performed unaccompanied doo-wop songs at Universal Studios Florida theme park.

Along with two other guys and a girl, he would sing out in front of a 1950s diner doing up to six shows a day, performing *a cappella* 1950s music to entertain the tourists.

Chris remained with the group for more than three years. Finally, he decided that if he really wanted to succeed in the music industry, he should form his own singing group. He recruited Joey Fatone, who also worked at Universal, in 1995. He called Justin Timberlake who turned him on to JC Chasez. Eventually, the group added Lance Bass as their fifth member. 'N Sync's first year together

wasn't easy. The group rehearsed their act in an empty warehouse for four or five hours a day.

It had no air conditioning and it was very, very hot. The boys were also increasingly frustrated in their attempts to find a manager or record company that would represent them. As both Chris and Joey retained their jobs at Universal Studios, Chris also had the extra burden of trying to keep up his grades in his college courses at Rollins. Finally he realized that he didn't have time to go to college and rehearse with the group. He had reached a fork in the road of his life, and he had to make a choice.

Fortunately for Chris, it was a very lucky gamble.

'N Sync's first year together wasn't easy. The group rehearsed their act in an empty warehouse for four or five hours a day.

A Lucky Guy

Brown-eyed Chris has a lot of nicknames. He's been variously called 'Lucky,' 'Psycho,' 'Crazy' and 'Puerto Rico' by the other band members (the latter due to his Spanish heritage). No matter what they choose to call him, all the other 'N Sync boys confess that it's the wild and hyper Chris who always keeps them laughing. Lance professes to never having seen him sleep! Perhaps that's a bit of an overstatement, but with Chris you never know!

Justin has said that Chris's manic energy has been a real asset to 'N Sync, providing a lift whenever they get tired. As soon as he gets on stage, Chris is fired up by the crowd, and by the sheer excitement of performing live.

Like Justin and JC, Chris loves to play basketball and despite his size (he stands 5ft 9in tall), he's pretty good.

He's also a big fan of football and hockey. Chris remains loyal to his hometown teams: the Pittsburgh Steelers are his number one American football team and he supports the Pittsburgh Penguins hockey team.

One of the reasons that Chris chose to go to college in Florida was its year-long sunny weather. Beach season just never seemed to last long enough for him in the Northeast! Of course, now that 'N Sync have made it big, Chris doesn't see the beach as much as he'd like, but he still tries to catch as much sun and sand as possible when he's home. An avid surfer, Chris admits that the most thrilling (and potentially dangerous) thing he's ever done was surfing the waves off Orlando during a hurricane.

Chris is the sole member of the group who still has enough energy for nightlife after performing. While the

other 'N Sync guys might head off to bed after a show, Chris is still ready to go. He loves club-hopping and exploring the hot spots in a new city. He doesn't even care what type of music is playing—if there's dancing, he's there!

Although Chris complains that one of his main faults is his short attention span, he's actually very patient about sitting down and writing notes to his fans. To make the job easier, he recently purchased a laptop computer which he carries with him all over the world. Believe it or not, his e-mail address has become common knowledge among some of 'N Sync's fans. He admits that he gave it out to a few fans, who passed it on, and now it's chaos! He tries to reply to his e-mails as much as he can, but realizes there's only so much he can do.

Don't let Chris fool you, he's very devoted. Some days when he downloads the contents of his electronic mailbox, he can have as many as 300 letters from fans. He doesn't mind though. He likes keeping in touch with the people who have made 'N Sync such a worldwide success.

While the other 'N Sync guys might head off to bed after a show, Chris is still ready to go. He loves club-hopping and exploring the hot spots in a new city.

Walk On The Wild Side

Since becoming a hit at home, Chris has more of a hard time going out unnoticed by 'N Sync's luckiest fans. He admits that it's probably his wild hair that attracts all the attention!

Fortunately, cheerful Chris doesn't usually mind signing a couple of autographs or posing for a photo, even when doing so will make him late for the movies.

When it comes to the ladies, talkative Chris doesn't have any trouble striking up a conversation, but the other guys claim that he has a fear of commitment that prevents his relationships from lasting very long. He's been in love twice—the first was Kelly, a girl he dated in high school, the other was Catherine, who was his steady companion for three months. It was the longest romance of his life!

What sort of girl makes Chris take notice? Well, considering how wild and silly he can be sometimes, it is no surprise that he finds talkative, funny girls attractive. He admits that he's drawn to a pretty face and a spunky personality. Furthermore, if a girl can throw caution to the wind and be spontaneous, he's thrilled to be her partner in adventure.

As every 'N Sync fan knows, Chris has his own personal style that's unique. But that wasn't always the case. During 'N Sync's first tour of Europe, the group habitually dressed in the same clothing. That made Chris very uncomfortable as he's committed to a more casual style. Being a jeans and T-shirts type of guy, he admits he felt very uncomfortable in matching suits that 'N Sync used to wear. Fortunately these days 'N Sync have changed their look enough to allow their individual styles to shine through. The guys have even become used to Chris's unusual fashion statements. In early 1998, when he found an Orlando stylist who specialized in the braids that have since become his trademark, no one in the group even blinked!

For Chris, as well as the other members of 'N Sync, their success has been a dream come true. It's even more satisfying for him to know that he brought the group together.

When he's in the mood for fast food, Chris heads over to Taco Bell ☆ Two of his best-loved movies are *Star Wars* and the Adam Sandler comedy *Happy Gilmore* ☆ Chris's prized possession is an autographed photo of Karate master Bruce Lee. ☆ He is afraid of heights ☆ No Doubt lead singer Gwen Stefani is Chris's dream girl ☆ One of his goals is to never cut his hair again! ☆ Chris boasts that he has a pet tree, named Tree ☆ He doesn't own a car. Instead, Chris uses his in-line skates to get around town ☆ Chris thinks his feet are too small ☆ He enjoys reading fantasy novels ☆ No cola drinks for Chris—he prefers milk and orange juice ☆ His prized possession is his enormous collection of vinyl albums ☆ Chris rates Mel Gibson and George Clooney as two of the best actors around ☆ The animated TV series *South Park* makes Chris laugh ☆

US Discography

Singles

'I Want You Back'
Released March 1998
Highest Chart Position: 13

'Tearin' Up My Heart'
Released July 1998
Highest Chart Position: 5

'Merry Christmas, Happy Holidays'
Released November 1998

Albums

'N Sync
Released April 1998
Highest Chart Position: 2
Tearin' Up My Heart/I Just Want To Be With You/Here We Go/I Want You Back/
For The Girl Who Has Everything/Everything I Own/I Drive Myself Crazy/God Must
Have Spent A Little More Time On You/Crazy For You/Sailing/You Got It/Giddy Up/
I Need Love

Home For Christmas
Released November 1998
Home For Christmas/Under My Tree/I Never Knew The Meaning Of Christmas/Merry
Christmas, Happy Holidays/The Christmas Song (Chestnuts Roasting)/I Guess It's
Christmas Time/All I Want Is You/The First Noel/In Love On Christmas/It's
Christmas/Oh Holy Night/Love's In Our Hearts On Christmas Day/The Only Gift/
Kiss Me At Midnight